100

Unexplored

Beaches

100 Top beaches in the world

100 Ultimate Escape

By : Gala Publication

2

Published By :

Gala Publication

© Copyright 2015 – Gala Publication

ISBN-13: **978-1519533623**
ISBN-10: **1519533624**

Table of Contents

Chapter 3: Unusual Beaches You Won't Believe Exist.................................103

8

Chapter 1:
Preface

A beach is made of very small loose rock (sand) that gathers at the shore of a body of water. Beaches are created by waves or currents. The sand comes from erosion of rocks both far away from and near the water. Coral reefs are a major source of sand.

A beach's shape depends on how the waves move. Some waves move material up the beach, while others move it down the beach. On sandy beaches, the waves move sand away from the beach, making gentle slopes.

When the waves are not strong enough to move the sand away, the beach is steeper.

Crabs, insects, and birds feed on material left by the waves. Some small animals dig into the sand to get their food. Birds use beaches to nest, and sea turtles lay their eggs on ocean beaches. Sea grasses and other beach plants grow on areas of the beach and dunes where there is not much activity.

Beach is seen as a place of relaxation because it is normally quiet and peaceful there. To look around you and see the beauty of mother nature at it's finest. The majority of people you ask will say that it is one of their favorite vacation destinations. Not only for the beauty and relaxation but for the sheer entertainment, playing water sports in the ocean, playing volleyball or Frisbee on the shore, or just plain relaxing and being lazy by laying in a hammock with a drink in your hand.

Chapter 2:
Best Beaches Around The World

Anse Lazio, Praslin, Seychelle

Anse Lazio, on the northwest tip of Praslin island, is known widely as the most beautiful beach in the Seychelles and is by far the most photographed. It's no wonder: The beach is long and broad with velvety sand and shocking blue water, and it's fringed with swaying palms and leafy takamaka trees. To add to the drama, it's also framed by enormous granite boulders on either side.

Matira Beach, Bora Bora, French Polynesia

Matira is perhaps the most famous of Tahiti's beaches, and for good reason. The mile-long stretch of silky, powder-white sand slopes gently into a shallow emerald lagoon, and is backed by a thick curtain of palms and tropical foliage. Added bonus: It's one of the only public-access beaches in Bora Bora, so you won't need to pay five-star resort prices to enjoy its beauty.

Waipio Valley Beach, Big Island, Hawaii

This beach in Waipio Valley is one of the hardest to get to in Hawaii—you must hike or drive down a treacherously narrow, steep road to reach your destination. But it's well worth the trek: At the bottom, you're rewarded with a mile-long black volcanic sand beach bordered by 2000-foot cliff walls and backed by thick rainforest. If that weren't scenic enough, the Kaluahine and Waiulili waterfalls cut into the cliffs at the south end of the beach, and are accessible via a boulder-strewn trail along the surf.

Honopu Beach, Kauai, Hawaii

Also known as Cathedral Beach, Honopu—like Waipio Valley—is quite difficult to reach. For starters, it's not accessible except by water, so to get there you must swim from an offshore boat, or from neighboring Kalalau Beach (a quarter-mile swim). But the trouble is worth it: Think cumin-colored sand bordered by soaring, vegetation-cloaked cliffs—and, most times, not a soul in sight. Fun fact: It's served as a location on such films as Six Days, Seven Nights, Raiders of the Lost Ark, and King Kong.

Honokalani Beach, Wai'anapanapa State Park, Maui, Hawaii

With its jet-black shore, lapis lazuli waters and thick, jungle-like foliage, Honokalani Beach is a photographer's dream. Besides lying lazily on the "sand"—actually made up of of tiny lava pebbles—there's plenty to do: you'll find seaside lava tubes and sea caves carved into the lava cliffs along the shore. It's wild, unspoiled Hawaii at its best, and a necessary stop en route to Hana.

El Castillo, Tulum, Riviera Maya, Mexico

When it comes to Mexican beaches, this one can't be beat: It hugs the base of towering, 40-foot limestone cliffs. Its pale, silvery sand leads invitingly into the clear, shallow Caribbean Sea, and it's flanked by palms and lush vegetation on either side. Best of all, it's located directly beneath the famous El Castillo ruins, which can be admired from the shore.

Fraser Island, Queensland, Australia

Australia is known for its spectacular beaches, including this stunning colored beach on Fraser Island. For starters, the entire island is World Heritage-listed for being the largest sand island in the world. Its golden sand beach is backed by fiery bronze cliffs; further beyond, you'll find lush rainforest rich with native wildlife. It's of equal beauty—and far less touristed—than the more famous Whitehaven Beach and the Great Barrier Reef at large.

Lopes Mendes, Ilha Grande, Brazil

Forget Rio: Lopes Mendes is two miles of unspoiled, deserted, powder-white sand that leads to some of the world's clearest, most crystalline waters. There are no beach shacks or restaurants here; instead, you'll find thick, wild sea shrub, almond trees, and squat palms, perfect for napping beneath. It's quite a trek—a three-hour drive to Angra dos Reis from Rio, then a ferry, then a taxi-boat, then a short hike through a forest—but well worth the effort.

Blinky Beach, Lord Howe Island, Australia

While many of the continent's best beaches can be found in Queensland, make no mistake—New South Wales firmly holds it own. Besides its excellent surf, Blinky Beach, on the east side of Lord Howe Island, is fantastically beautiful: It's situated between Blinky Point and a promontory known as Mutton Bird Lookout, and boasts the requisite powder-white sand and azure waters. Behind it, you'll find tall dunes dotted with prickly spinifex and wild daisies.

El Nido, Palawan, Philippines

Shockingly, Palawan has remained steadily under the radar, and we certainly hope it stays that way. El Nido alone is home to around 50 white sand beaches—it's impossible to choose just one—all of which are set around dramatic limestone formations and boast the finest and whitest sand you'll ever see. The water is so blindingly blue it makes the Caribbean Sea look murky in comparison, and the sunsets? Well, they'll ruin you for life. Consider yourself warned.

Anse Source D'Argent, La Digue Island, Seychelles

Anse Source d'Argent is the most popular beach in the island of La Digue in Seychelles. This stunning strip of shoreline features powdery sand, gigantic boulders and swaying palm trees. Visitors need to pay an admission fee to enter the beach but one peek at the blue azure waters and you'll decide it's worth it.

Crane Beach, Barbados

Crane Beach has been named to many 'Best Beaches' list, and deservedly so. With its powder-soft sand, crystal-clear waters and and picturesque views of jagged cliffs, the beach is postcard-ready. The spot is a favorite for adventurous types. The lively waves are perfect for boogie boarding and body surfing.

Salomon Bay Beach, St. John, U.S. Virgin Islands

One of the best beaches on St. John, Salomon Bay Beach has soft white sand, shade, shallow water entry and sparkling waters in an unbelievable aquamarine hue. It also has an off-the-beaten-path location that makes it attractive to those looking for a hidden gem--visitors need to hike a trail to get to this postcard-perfect spot.

Baia do Sancho, Fernando de Noronha, Brazil

Baia do sancho, located in the Fernando de Noronha archipelago, is appealing for a number of reasons, including the sparkling emerald water, the coral reefs and the solitude, according to Fodors. To get to this terrestrial paradise, trekkers have to follow a dirt trail , climb down a rickety ladder through the rock wall, throught a tight crevasse, down an even ricketier ladder, and finally down a frozen uneven, slippery-sandy steps,'said forbes .

Flamenco Beach, Culebra, Puerto Rico

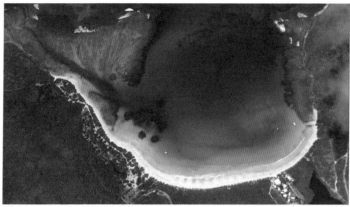

An aerial view of Flamenco Beach in Puerto Rico. Generally regarded as Puerto Rico's best beach, Flamenco Beach stretched for a mile around a sheltered, horseshoe-shaped bay. It's known for its superb swimming, sport fishing and diving sites.

Maya Bay, Ko Phi Phi, Thailand

A stunningly beautiful bay that's sheltered by high cliffs on three sides, Maya Bay in Ko Phi Phi has attracted tourists since it was featured in the movie 'The Beach.' The beaches here boast silky soft white sand, and colorful coral and exotic fish in exceptionally clear water. The area is so beautiful, however, that the beaches can get crowded

White Beach, Boracay, Philippines

Located in Malay, Aklan, Western Visayas in the Philippines, Boracay has been named 'world's best island' numerous times. It's easy to see why with its stretches of powder-white sand beaches, crystal-clear waters and thriving nightlife

Etretat Plage, France

Best known for its twin white cliffs and pebbly beach, Étretat is a popular tourist destination. It has also attracted and inspired artists and writers. Its dramatic landscape was painted by Claude Monet in the 19th century.

Grace Bay Beach, Providenciales, Turks and Caicos

Located on the north shore of Providenciales (or 'Provo') in Turks and Caicos, Grace Bay Beach stretches for several miles. With its crystal-clear, turquoise and sapphire waters, and white power-soft sand, it's considered one of the most spectacular beaches in the world. 'It's the beach postcards are made from,' said a TripAdvisor member.

Grand Anse Beach, St. George, Grenada

Described by Frommer's as 'the granddaddy' of Grenada's 45 beaches, Grand Anse Beach has two miles of 'sugar white sand fronting a sheltered bay,' a postcard-perfect setting topped off by clear, azure waters. Many visitors never leave this part of the island--there are many activities to keep them occupied, from parasailing to windsurfing.

Trunk Bay, St. John, U.S. Virgin Islands

Trunk Bay is part of the Virgin Islands National Park and offers visitors beautiful, pristine beaches and warm waters. U.S. News recommends the Underwater Trail — a snorkeling path of coral and fish with underwater plaques.

Navagio Beach, Greece

Navagio Beach or Shipwreck Beach, is an exposed cove on the coast of Zakynthos, in the Ionian Islands of Greece. The area is defined by its sheer limestone cliffs, white sand beaches, and clear blue water, which attract thousands of tourists yearly.

Twin Beaches of Nacpan and Calitang, El Nido, Palawan, Philippines

El Nido in Palawan, Philippines has many beautiful beaches but the 'twin beaches' of Nacpan and Calitang (they share the same shoreline) are especially unique. Located in a remote town (a 45-minute drive from El Nido), the spot is still relatively unspoiled and undeveloped, making it a 'hidden gem.' Climb a hill for the perfect panoramic shot of the stunning beaches.

Luskentyre Beach, Scotland

Located on the west coast of South Harris in the Outer Hebrides, Luksentyre boasts miles of white sand and stunning turquoise waters, and has been voted ones of the best beaches in the UK. It also makes for a romantic spot, and stormy skies make the views even more dramatic

Balos Beach, Crete, Greece

Many consider Balos Beach the most stunning beach in Crete but reaching it requires quite an arduous trek, via car on a rough road and then a walk down a goat path (boat trips are available). But visitors to this spectacular landscape say the pilgrimage is worth it. One TripAdvisor user said: 'The photos don't do [Balos Beach] justice.'

Praia Dona Ana, Lagos, Portugal

One of the most photographed beaches in the Algarve region of Portugal, the small cove of Praia Dona Ana has golden sand and crystalline waters, surrounded by steep, colorful cliffs and grottoes. Visitors can climb to the cliff to enjoy spectacular views of the rock formations and the blue water.

Magens Bay, St. Thomas, U.S. Virgin Islands

St. Thomas's most popular beach, this beautiful one-mile stretch is a public park and was donated to the people of the Virgin Islands by Arthur Fairchild. The water is usually very calm in this heart-shaped protected bay. The beach property also includes a coconut grove, a mangrove, and an arboretum.

Rabbit Island Beach, Lampedusa, Italy

Visitors trek to the sun-bleached island of Lampedusa, the last trace of Italian terrain before the African coast to scuba dive and relax in its beaches. One of its prettiest beaches can be found on Rabbit Island, which boast soft sand, clear aquamarine waters and spectacular views

Padang Padang Beach, Bali, Indonesia

A popular surf point in Bali, Padang Padang Beach can get crowded (especially after being featured in the movie 'Eat, Pray, Love.') But with its stunning views to the Indian Ocean and spectacular sunsets, there's no denying its beauty. To get to the bustling beach, visitors walk past monkeys and down a narrow staircase built between a cliff face.

Pigeon Point Beach, Tobago, Trinidad and Tobagao

Located in southwest Tobago, Pigeon Point Beach charges a fee for entrance to their shores, according to U.S. News. But visitors who get to step foot on its bone-white sand and take a dip in its sparking aquamarine water don't mind. A TripAdvisor user says: 'Speechless. The beach is so gorgeous, extremely picturesque ... and just beautiful.'

Piha Beach, North Island, New Zealand

Piha Beach is one of the most popular beaches of Auckland's wild west coast, and with its laid-back vibe awesome surf which rolls in over the Tasman Sea, it's a great place to go surfing. Day trippers are also drawn here by the vast stretch of volcanic black sand framed by dramatic rocky terrain.

Seven Mile Beach, Grand Cayman, Cayman Islands

Tourists sailing off Seven Mile Beach in Grand Cayman, Cayman Islands. Frequently cited as one of the best beaches of the Caribbean, Seven Mile Beach is home to soft-coral sand and some of Grand Cayman's best resorts.

Playa de Ses Illetes, Formentera, Spain

A popular day trip to Ibiza , the island of formentera is known for its stunning beaches . but many consider de ses Illetes the best in the island, if not in Spain. one trip advisor user says, "hypnotizing. I have been to plenty of beaches around the world(and have)never seen such beauty . The color of the water would change by each step I took.. I saw seven colors of blue

Boulders Beach, Simon's Town, South Africa

A sheltered beach made up of inlets between granite boulders, Boulders Beach in Simon's Town in South Africa is also home to a colony of African penguins that established there in the 1980s. Wooden walkways allow tourists to view the penguins in their natural habitat, and going about their daily business: sunning, waddling on the sand and diving into the waters.

Laughing Bird Caye National Park, Belize

Laughing Bird Caye is the most popular day trip from Placencia in southern Belize. The island is what many consider the perfect tropical paradise, sand and palm trees surrounded by shallow coral reef perfect for snorkeling or diving.

Lumahai Beach, Kauai, Hawaii

You'll find Lumahai Beach the star of many postcards, paintings and even movies--it was made famous in the movie South Pacific. While it is one of the most stunning and picturesque beaches in Hawaii, it is not recommended for swimming, due to its strong currents.

Beau Vallon Beach, Mahe, Seychelles

The largest and most popular beach in Mahe, Seychelles, Beau Vallon is known as a base for diving and snorkeling due to its clear waters and coral reefs. Located in the northwestern coast of the island, the beach boasts white sand and clear, calm water perfect for swimming.

Nha Trang Beach, Vietnam

Nha Trang's golden-sand beach is the jewel of this Vietnamese city. It boasts turquoise waters, where various sections are designated for swimmers, according to Lonely Planet. Nha Trang is a popular spot for diving enthusiasts and may be the only spot on the central coast where you can find certified dive shops.

Long Beach, Perhentian Islands, Malaysia

Perhentian Kecil, off the northeastern coast of Malaysia, is one of the most popular backpacker islands in Southeast Asia. Most flock to Long Beach, which features fine, white sand and excellent swimming. It is also home to many budget hotels and nightlife spots.

Navio Beach, Vieques, Puerto Rico

Framed by cliffs, palm trees and other native plants, Navio Beach is one place not to miss in Puerto Rico. Surrounded by cliffs and lined with lush sea grape trees, the beach also features hidden caves just waiting to be explored. Navio's lively waves make it an ideal spot for beginning surfers and boogie boarders.

Malolo Island, Fiji

This intimate Fijian resort features golden sandy beaches, abundant coral reefs, swaying coconut palms and azure seas. In short, paradise. Active visitors can enjoy diving, waterskiing, and island hopping

Ninety Mile Beach, North Island, New Zealand

Te Oneroa-a-Tōhē, also known as the Ninety Mile Beach, is a famous stretch of sand, reminiscent of a desert landscape, that stretches from just west of Kaitaia right to Cape Reinga, the northernmost tip of New Zealand, according to CNN.

Muri Beach, Cook Islands

The Cook Islands, a set of 15 islands in the heart of the South Pacific spread over an area the size of India, is known for its sparkling blue lagoons, white sand beaches and rugged mountainous interiors. The lagoon is at its deepest around Muri, making it an ideal spot for swimming, snorkeling and boating

Cable Beach, Broome, Australia

Cable Beach, at Broome in Western Australia's Kimberley region, is a 13 mile-long stretch of pure white sand, set against a backdrop of red ochre cliffs and fringed by the turquoise waters of the Indian Ocean. It's known for its spectacular sunsets, the perfect time to ride a camel along the beach.

Beaches of Manuel Antonio National Park, Costa Rica

Located in the mid-Pacific coast of Costa Rica, just south of the city of Quepos, Manuel Antonio National Park features four primary beaches with white sand, clear-blue water and stunning views. The park itself is home to 109 species of mammals and 184 species of birds, including white-faced and howler monkeys, two- and three-toed sloths and iguanas.

El Cabo San Juan Beach, Tayrona National Park, Colombia

One of the many beaches located inside Colombia's Tayrona National Park, the palm-fringed El Cabo San Juan Beach is perhaps the most picturesque. Rocky outcroppings serve as ideal lookouts but don't miss the cabin, located right on the sea which offers beautiful views of the beach and the park itself.

Beaches of Belitung Island, Sumatra, Indonesia

The island of Belitung, located on the east coast of Sumatra, Indonesia, is home to several white-sand beaches that make it a perfect resort destination. Many of the best beaches are on the north side of the island. One of them, Tanjung Tinggi Beach, features perfect sand and boulders that visitors can climb.

Playa Del Amor, Marietas Islands, Mexico

One of the most popular attractions in Puerto Vallarta in Mexico is the stunning 'hidden beach' in the Marieta Islands. The site was formed by a collapse of the volcanic rock that makes up the island. Over time, a cave was created by the sea; and visitors have to swim through the tunnel in the cave to access the beach.

Playa Paraiso, Tulum, Mexico

Located just north of the Tulum ruins, Playa Paraiso is a great beach to try out various water activities, including snorkeling and scuba diving. It's not a secluded beach but visitors will enjoy the views, the sugar-like sand, and huge palm trees. There are also hammocks, lounges and umbrellas available.

Glyfada Beach, Corfu, Greece

With its long stretches of white sand, tree-covered cliffs, and stunning rock formations, Glyfada Beach is considered to be the best in Corfu, according to U.S. News. For visitors wanting to spend more time in the area, Glyfada has many water sports facilities, shops and restaurants.

Praia das Rodas, Las Islas Cies, Galicia, Spain

Located on Las Islas Cies, an uninhabited and pristine national park (open to the public only in summer), Praia das Rodas features a 'perfect crescent of soft, pale sand backed by small dunes sheltering a calm lagoon of crystal-clear sea,' according to the Guardian

Knip Beach, Curacao

Popular with both locals and tourists, Knip Beach some of the most picturesque views in Curacao. The beach is used as a starting point for snorkeling, due to the presence of a coral reef nearby.

Nissi Beach, Ayia Napa, Cyprus

Nissi Beach is the most popular beach in the Ayia Napa area and on the island of Cyprus. The beach has golden sands and the waters are clean and clear. It is possible to walk out for up to a 100m without the water passing your waist.

Constance Halaveli Resort, North Ari Atoll, Maldives

The Constance Halaveli, set in the North Ari Atoll of the Maldives in the Indian Ocean, is a dream destination. The beaches boast crystal waters and sparkling sand, and the views feature lush foliage and overwater villas. This is also an ideal area for diving, with colorful marine fauna and sealife.

Essaouira Beach, Morocco

Looking to surf on your beach vacation? Morocco's Essaouira Beach has perfect conditions for the beginning surfer. The beach has a soft sand bottom is best at high tide with light north wind, according to CompleteMorocco.com.

Sunrise Beach, Ko Lipe, Thailand

This idyllic spit of sand curves gently into turquoise water on an island in the far south of Thailand, towards Malaysia. Ko Lipe has become a party destination in recent years but still retains a laid-back atmosphere with many delightful tropical coves. Sunset Beach - on the opposite side of the island - is also popular later in the day, for self-explanatory reasons.

Negril, Jamaica

As one of the largest and most well known beach resorts in Jamaica you're sure to get your share of rest and relaxation as you take in the laid back atmosphere.

Langkawi, Malaysia

Meaning "land of one's wishes" this beach paradise was once reputed to be a notorious pirate hideout.

Cape Cod, Massachusetts

With sparkling sand and blue water the "arm" of Massachusetts attracts thousands of visitors to its National Seashore. It's also not that hard to get to the well known islands of Martha's Vineyard or Nantucket from here.

Nungwi, Zanzibar

Found near the north tip of Zanzibar this white sand beach off Africa's east coast is dotted with fishing villages and is home to a diverse variety of marine life.

Red Beach, Greece

To get here you can either take a <u>boat</u> or descend along a steep path leading down the side of the cliff in the background. Although the island of Santorini isn't really popular for its beaches, this one is too unique to disappoint.

Sidari, Greece

Found on the Greek island of Corfu, some of this beaches most recognizable landmarks are the unusual cliff formations known as the canal d amour (channel of love). According to legend if a couple swims together in the surrounding water they'll be together forever.

The Baths, Virgin Gorda, British Virgin Islands

The Baths are situated at the southern tip of Virgin Gorda, the third largest island of the British Virgin Islands. Huge granite boulders lie in piles on the beach, forming spectacular tunnels and grottoes that are open to the sea and flood at high tide. The sandy beaches are lined with tropical palms, adding to the dramatic effect.

Zlatni Rat, Croatia

Zlatni Rat (Golden Cape) is among Europe's most famous beaches and one of the top tourist <u>attractions in Croatia</u>. Situated near the city of Bol on the southern coast of the island of Brac, Zlatni Rat is a narrow white pebble beach. The amazing shape of the beach shifts with the changes in tide, currents and wind. In 2009, it was named as one of the top ten best beaches in the world by Lonely Planet.

Oludeniz, Turkey

Ölüdeniz is a small village located on the south west coast of Turkey on the Aegean Sea. It has a secluded sandy bay at the mouth of Ölüdeniz, on a blue lagoon. This beach is famous for its shades of turquoise and remains one of the most photographed beaches on the Mediterranean. Ölüdeniz is also regarded as one of the best places in the world to paraglide due to its unique panoramic views.

Panama City Beach, Florida, United States

Featuring 27 miles of white sand beaches along the turquoise waters of the Gulf of Mexico, Panama City Beach is home to two State Parks, dozens of public beach access points, waterfront restaurants that serve up fresh local seafood, and legendary attractions. The waters here are famous with fishermen and scuba divers who enjoy the benefits of dozens artificial reefs located offshore, and with a coastline that angles slightly toward the west, in Panama City Beach you can watch the sunset over the Gulf of Mexico every day of the year.

Diani Beach, Kenya

Diani Beach is a major beach resort on the Indian Ocean coast of Kenya. It is located 30 kilometres south of Mombasa, in the nearby Kwale County. The beach is about 10 kilometres long, from the Kongo river to the north and Galu beach to the south, the sparkling white sands and lush greenery of Diani invite you to relax under a beach umbrella with a refreshing drink. Try a camel ride for the tourist experience or book a bike tour inland for a glimpse of life in local villages. Diani is also a base for several safari companies.

Placencia Beach, Belize, Central America

Placencia is a gorgeous emerald peninsula in southern Belize with 16 miles of sandy beaches. The Caribbean sea is to the east and the charming Placencia lagoon lies to west looking to the mountains on the mainland. Placencia is essentially divided into two parts: south of the airstrip and north of the airstrip. The entire peninsula can be easily navigated on a beach cruiser bike. The busy part of Placencia lies in the south where the visitor will find the greater concentration of coffee shops, bistros, internet cafes, the harbor, guest houses, taxi and bus station, banks and local restaurants.

Warwick Long Bay, Bermuda

Warwick Long Bay beach is a long and magnificent half a mile stretch of pink sands. Against a backdrop of grape & cedar trees, and low grasses, the beach looks fabulous. It's one of the most picturesque beaches of Bermuda. Warwick Long Bay lies on South Shore Park in Warwick parish and to the east of Horseshoe bay beach. The beach is full of little coves and rocks. The main entrance to the beach is at the west end (i.e. right side as you face the water). A short road winds down from the car park.

Bottom Bay, Barbados

Tucked away on the south coast, past the Crane Beach and Sam Lord's Castle is **Bottom Bay**, a wide expansive beach with smooth rolling waves riding onto the shore.

The beach is semi enclosed by high coral cliffs, providing a panoramic view of the south shore. The scene is completed by the presence of tall palm trees that add to the peaceful and relaxing atmosphere of the bay.

Always a popular picnic spot, it is also becoming a popular place to live and a number of homes are being built on the tops of the cliffs overlooking the beach and ocean. People who live there report spotting turtles and whales in the waters below the rocks.

Unawatuna, Sri Lanka

Unawatuna is a cautionary tale for the rest of Sri Lanka's south coast. Where there was once a flawless crescent of golden sand that swept along a palm-lined shore with turquoise waters that had just enough surf to make for ideal swimming conditions, there is now one of Sri Lanka's less appealing beach towns.

The beautiful water is still there and you can still find decent patches of sand, but in several places greed has replaced good taste and common sense. Bulldozers have pushed huge boulders right up to and beyond the high tide line, allowing for the construction of some especially ugly hotels and cafes. Ironically, authorities have actually enforced setbacks on the west half of Unawatuna's beach and the result is much more salubrious.

Unawatuna makes for a good, quick beach escape from Galle's Fort: it's only 6km southeast. Otherwise it offers a cheap and cheerful sandy idyll, at least on the bulldozer- and boulder-free west end.

Los Roques, Venezuela

Los Roques is an archipelago of Venezuela, located in the

Caribbean, at 168 Km (100 miles) north of La Guaira, Caracas´ port. For its beauty and ecological importance it was declared national park in 1972 to protect a marine ecosystem of exceptional beauty and ecological value dominated by **coral reefs,mangroves**, and **seagrass beds**. It is without a doubt one of the most beautiful natural areas of Venezuela. The park, located about 80 miles (128 km) north of the port of "La Guaira" in Caracas, covers 221,120 hectares (546 acres), making it the largest marine park in the Caribbean Sea.

The coral reefs host some of the most beautiful underwater fauna and flora of the Caribbean. The park has exceptionally beautiful beaches of white sand and multicolor, crystalline warm waters which make it a diving, sailing and fishing paradise.

Cala Agulla, Majorca, Spain

Cala Agulla in the north-east of Mallorca boasts fine, golden-brown sand, perfect for a game of beach volleyball, and a surrounding pine forest. 520 metres long, it averages a width of 50 metres. Best accessed from Capdepera, 1.8km away, travel in the direction of Cala Ratjada before turning at the signpost which takes you to a pay-to-use car park.

PORTHCURNO,UK

he closest Britain gets to beach paradise in Cornwall, with turquoise waters that glint in the sunshine and fine yellow sand. High cliffs on either side enclose and protect the bay, and it's also overlooked by the famous open-air Minack Theatre. The swimming is great, too, with kiddies safe in shallow pools and experienced swimmers catered for by the steep shelf and deep water.

FALSTERBO,SWEDEN

A chic and smart beach resort on the southwestern tip of Sweden, Falsterbo has ridiculously white sand – bring your sunglasses to avoid the glare – and the cutest beachside huts you'll ever see. It's a very peaceful and sedate spot, thanks to the ban on jet skis and motorboats, and excellent ice cream shops are never far away.

PALANGA,LITHUANIA

Palanga is the busiest and most popular seaside resort in Lithuania, and the reason is its large, sandy beach and glorious, undulating sand dunes. If you like parties, come here in the summer (June–September), when the resort's population explodes and the beach parties never stop.

TROIA,PORTUGAL

Portugal does pure, unadulterated beach extremely well. And Troia, stretching 18km just south of Lisbon, is no exception. Kick off your sandals and sink your feet into the soft sand, dive into the inviting waves or enjoy watching dolphins cavorting not far from shore.

BUTTERFLYVALLEY,TURKEY

Beautiful Butterfly Valley is difficult to access – a steep walk down cliffs or a boat trip – but all this contributes to its undeveloped charm. A deep canyon licked by azure water, it's named for its fluttery inhabitants who appear between June and September. If you can't quite tear yourself away, it's possible to stay overnight in basic wooden huts.

SYLT,GERMANY

Sylt's nickname, the "German Hamptons" speaks volumes for the place: genteel and sophisticated, with a clientele to match, the island on Germany's North Sea coast has a fabulously long stretch of immaculate beach. If posh restaurants and glitzy boutiques aren't your thing, escape to the sand dunes with a bucket and spade.

GOLDEN SANDS,BULGARIA

Bulgaria's best seaside resort, with the purest sand and very clear water. Big and boisterous with a casino, mini-golf, water parks, fairground rides and all the accompanying hotels and bars, the resort is an extremely popular summer spot for Bulgarians.

BRELA,CROATIA

With its long coastline and diminutive islands, it's no surprise that Croatia is a veritable honey pot of beaches – each one vying for position of best beach. Bol on the island of Brac might be the most famous, but little Brela, on the mainland opposite, is a less touristy, more relaxed option, studded with private coves fringed with pine trees.

ELAFONISI,CRETE

A strawberries-and-cream beach, with gorgeous pinky
sand that's made of thousands of broken shells. It lines
the "island" of Elafonisi, the southwesternmost point of
Crete; certain bits are busier than others, but it's perfectly
possible to find a quiet and secluded cove – azure waters
and baby-soft sand are the rewards for your search.

RAINBOW BEACH, QUEENSLAND

Enormous Rainbow Beach, in southeastern Queensland, gets its name from its surrounding colourful sand dunes – a mixture of browns, blacks, oranges, yellows and reds – that are said to have been formed by a rainbow-coloured spirit plunging into the cliffs following a battle with a wicked tribesman. In actual fact, the sand is simply rich in vibrant minerals like ilmenite, zircon and rutile.

PHRA NANG BEACH, Thailand

Accessible by longboat only, this secluded beach is backed by the cavernous Tham Phra Nang Nok, or "Princess Cave", believed by fishermen to be the home of a mythical sea princess. There are no restaurants on the beach – instead, look out for the longboats selling juices and snacks.

CAYO LARGO, Cuba

The highlights on Cuba's Cayo Largo (Large Island) are its two western beaches, Playa Sirena and Playa Paraiso, where warm shallow waters lap ribbons of pale, downy sand. Sirena is more geared up to tourism, with a café and watersports, while Paraiso is quieter and more private.

MATEMWE, ZANZIBAR

The traditional, palm-thatched fishing village of Matemwe, on the northeastern coast of Zanzibar, has a large, palm-fringed beach lined with a few quiet resorts. Just off shore is the Mnemba Atoll, home to some of the best scuba diving in East Africa. Sadly, the bucolic charm of the village and beach might not last much longer, as the walled enclosures of the larger resorts are beginning to intrude.

MYRTOS BEACH,KEFALONIA

Subject of many an iconic photograph, Myrtos Beach is regarded as the most dramatic beach in the Ionian islands – a splendid strip of dazzling, pure-white pebbles, laced by calm, turquoise water. Unsurprisingly, it attracts a fair number of visitors each day, and there's no shade to speak of, so bring a sun umbrella and a hat.

Kuta, Bali

Kuta Beach stretches for 8km, from the Balinese towns of Tuban to Petitenget, its huge and powerful waves thrashing onto its glorious white sand. Surfers are drawn here for the sport, while evenings are slightly more serene; the sunsets here are incredible – at their blood-red best in April, but streaky-pink at any time of year.

Eagle Beach, Aruba

With its clear and sparkling turquoise water and powder-soft white sand, it's no surprise that Eagle Beach on Aruba wins the prize for the most beautiful beach in the Caribbean. Watersports, swaying hammocks and luxury beachfront resorts complete the picture – it's the definition of paradise.

Mont Choisy Beach, Mauritius

The public beach of Mont Choisy is situated between Pointe aux Cannoniers and Mont Choisy and is almost 3 kilometers in length with white sand bends around the coast creating a bay of beautiful turquoise water, lined with the casuarina trees providing shade from the sun.

The beach might not be that busy during week days but during the weekend it is quite full. In case you are looking for a quieter and more intimate beach atmosphere make sure to visit the beach during the weekdays and not during the weekends.

Pereybere Beach, Mauritius

A small, but very busy, beach which is quite popular amongst Mauritian citizens for its cleanliness. The beach will not disappoint! If you walk across the rocks on the right you will find more secluded spots to sunbathe in privacy and even spot many tropical fish such as the angel fish.

Pereybere beach is full of life with fast food stalls spread along the beach selling kebab, sandwiches and also fresh pineapple. Also, few meters from the beach you will find many bars and restaurants serving Chinese, Mauritian and International cuisine.

Anse La Raie Beach, Mauritius

Anse La Raie Beach is located near the village of Calodyne, in the north of Mauritius. Several things can be said about Anse La Raie beach, but few visitors would probably consider this area as a beach as such.

Situated northwest of Calodyne, this area enjoys the same stunning views of the north Indian Ocean in a more peaceful and quiet environment. With clean and clear waters the lagoons offers great opportunities for both snorkelling and perhaps a bit of Mauritius kite surfing al dente!

For a better beach spot, head east of Anse La Raie. Park at Anse La Raie beach, cross the rocks to your northeast and walk along the coast, and you will find shallow waters and a small sandy beach. But still remain cautious the tide rises quickly there.

Le Morne Beach, Mauritius

Le Morne is situated on the south west tip of Mauritius and its beaches are located on the west part of the Le Morne peninsula on the foot of the Le Morne Brabant. The public beach of Le Morne is a lush beach surrounded by very clear waters providing great visibility without forgetting a magnificent landscape with Le Morne Mountain as an imposing background.

The Le Morne beach is particularly popular for windsurfing and kite surfers. The perfect wind conditions almost all year-round makes this beach one of the top kite and windsurfing destinations in the world. Swimming is also possible but you should always be cautious since kite surfers and surfers are always gliding on this lagoon.

Chapter 3:
Unusual Beaches You
Won't Believe Exist

Bowling Ball Beach, California

Compared to green sand or vanishing tides, "round rocks" don't initially sound like reason enough to visit this Californian beach. And yet, when you get down there and see the "bowling balls" sitting like some tidy giant's game on the sand, you can't help but get a thrill. Best seen at low tide, the rocks are freakily round and freakily regular, and clustered together as if they've been placed there. The truth is, they're stubborn. The softer rock around them washed away, but these tough customers withstood the waves.

Chandipur, India

The sea here has a magic trick: It disappears! At low tide it waves goodbye and heads out for some 5 km (yes, that's unusually far; when you see it happen you'll know how freaky it is). That in itself may not be enough to draw you here, but while you're waiting for the sea to come sloshing back in with a "just kidding!" you'll be able to explore the seabed, complete with shells, driftwood and little red crabs. And when you're in Orissa, why not check out some of its other off-the-tourist-trail beaches?

Vík Beach, Iceland

The little town of Vík has three distinctions. One, it's Iceland's southernmost point. Two, it's the rainiest place on the island. And three, it has one of the most beautiful beaches in the world. Obviously it's for looking at, rather than swimming in... White waves wash up on jet-black sands, like a beach scene in negative. The cliffs above glow green from all that rain. And strange basalt figures stand here and there like sculptures. They're traditionally believed to be ill-fated trolls that got caught out in the sun.

Glass Beach
MacKerricher State Park, Fort Bragg, California

The phrase "One man's trash is another man's treasure" has never been truer than at the glass beaches of MacKerricher State Park near Fort Bragg, California. The beaches were used as garbage dumps for nearly 60 years before conservation efforts began in 1967. Today, three of the beaches are filled with polished pieces of colorful glass. The beaches are open to tourists, but collecting the glass is prohibited.

Pink Sands Beach
Harbour Island, Bahamas

Miles of pink sand beaches stretch along the coast of Harbour Island in the Bahamas. The beaches get their color from red and pink shelled marine creatures called foraminifera that live in the coral reef off the island's coast.

Koekohe Beach
South Island, New Zealand

Maori legend has it that the Moeraki Boulders scattered along Koekohe Beach are the remains of eel baskets, gourds, and sweet potatoes from a large canoe wreck. The spherical rocks are the result of a natural process known as concretion, where grains of sand and stone combine to form these masses. Reaching a diameter of up to six feet, these boulders dot the eroded Otago coastline along the South Island of New Zealand.

Papakolea Beach
Kau, Hawaii

Located near the southernmost point on the big island of Hawaii, Papakolea Beach contains olive-colored sand. It gets its color from the erosion of the mineral olivine, which is found in the nearby volcanic debris. Papakolea Beach is one of only four green sand beaches in the world—the other three are located in Guam, Norway, and the Galapagos Islands.

Maho Beach
Saint Martin, island in the
northeast Caribbean

It's not turquoise waters or palm trees that make Maho
Beach on the Caribbean island of Saint Martin famous.
Instead, this beach's claim to fame is its location along
the flight path at Princess Juliana International Airport.
Due to an extremely short runway, planes landing at the
airport pass sunbathers at a considerably low altitude of
30–60 feet. Plane spotting along the beach is a popular
activity, so much so that local restaurants post flight
times for tourists to catch glimpses of the arriving planes.

Jökulsárlón
Vatnajökull National Park, Iceland

The black volcanic sands along the coast of this glacial lagoon provide a stark backdrop for the chunks of ice that wash ashore from a nearby glacier. Jökulsárlón and its frozen beach are considered a natural wonder of Iceland—it's no wonder it appeared in several major Hollywood movies, including Batman Begins and Die Another Day.

Whitehaven Beach
Queensland, Australia

Situated in the heart of the Great Barrier Reef are the
Whitsundays, a collection of 74 tropical islands off the
coast of Queensland, Australia. The most famous of the
island beaches is Whitehaven, mainly due to its dazzling
colors. The changing tide within Hill Inlet along the
northern end of the beach swirls around the white sands
and the blue ocean water, creating a lovely tie-dye effect.

Giant's Causeway
Antrim, Northern Ireland

The studded beach known as Giant's Causeway, a UNESCO World Heritage Site, is made up of polygonal columns of basalt protruding from the coast and water. They were caused by a volcanic eruption 60 million years ago, but one local legend claims that the columns were carved by a giant named Finn McCool (hence the name)

Red Sand Beach
Isla Rábida, Galapagos

Isla Rábida sits 600 miles off the coast of Ecuador in the Galapagos archipelago. This arid island has a human population of zero, but it's home to resident pink flamingos and sea lions. The coast of this volcanic island is famous for its red sand, which gets its color from the rocky coastal cliffs of oxidized lava.

Benagil Sea Cave
Algarve, Portugal

Accessible by boat, this sea cave in the Algarve region of Portugal hides a secluded beach. The area around Benagil Beach is full of limestone formations, but this renowned cave is the region's trophy and every photographer's dream.

Scala dei Turchi
Realmonte, Sicily

Resembling massive white stairs leading down to the ocean, the Scala dei Turchi (Stair of the Turks) is a tiered limestone beach cliff in southern Sicily. Located along the Realmonte coast, Scala dei Turchi only enhances an already gorgeous ocean view.

Shell Beach
Shark Bay, Australia

As its name implies, Shell Beach in the Shark Bay UNESCO World Heritage Site is made entirely of shells. One of the only beaches of this type in the world, it's comprised of nearly 70 miles of cockle shells along the L'Haridon Bight bay in Western Australia.

DISCLAIMER AND/OR LEGAL NOTICES: Every effort has been made to accurately represent this book and it's potential. Results vary with every individual, and your results may or may not be different from those depicted. No promises, guarantees or warranties, whether stated or implied, have been made that you will produce any specific result from this book. Your efforts are individual and unique, and may vary from those shown. Your success depends on your efforts, background and motivation.

The material in this publication is provided for educational and informational purposes only and is not intended as medical advice. The information contained in this book should not be used to diagnose or treat any illness, metabolic disorder, disease or health problem. Always consult your physician or health care provider before beginning any nutrition or exercise program. Use of the programs, advice, and information contained in this book is at the sole choice and risk of the reader.

22240831R00067

Printed in Great Britain
by Amazon